DR

DR

WHAT ARE THEY AND ...
THEY CAUSED

Third Edition 1903
C.W Leadbeater

New Edition 2019
Edited by Tarl Warwick

1

COPYRIGHT AND DISCLAIMER

FOREWORD

This is one of the earliest of several dozen notable booklets written by C.W. Leadbeater- one of the earliest students of Blavatsky and a notable early Theosophist. With a focus on experimentation, the opinions of this movement on dreams range from the more scientific to strictly mystic, from figure to figure and booklet to booklet; this one is primarily scientific (or at times pseudoscientific) and speaks of waking dreams, prediction by dreams, and symbolism in the same and a bit about the semi-malleable meanings. For those interested in dream interpretation itself there is not much here, but there's an extensive list of other literature by Leadbeaters' ideological contemporaries on various subjects.

Here we see an attempt to differentiate dream states into the physical, etheric, and astral- indeed, from the background of a Theosophist it is strictly necessary to do so, to divorce the mundanely physical dream in the cognitive sense from any further meaning. Of far greater (perhaps greatest) interest though are several related tales in this booklet about people who had dreams which seemed to predict future events, usually in a cautionary sense. As an anecdote, this has happened to me numerous times, and I may need to write my own work on my experience with dreams at some future date.

This edition of "Dreams" has been carefully edited for format and content. Care has been taken to retain all original intent and meaning.

DREAMS

CHAPTER I: INTRODUCTORY

Many of the subjects with which our Theosophical studies bring us into contact are so far removed from the experiences and interests of everyday life, that while we feel drawn towards them by an attraction which increases in geometrical progression as we come to know more of them and understand them better, we are yet conscious, at the back of our minds, as it were, of a faint sense of unreality, or at least impracticality, while we are dealing with them. When we read of the formation of the solar system, or even of the rings and rounds of our own planetary chain, we cannot but feel that, interesting though this is as an abstract study, useful as it is in showing us how man has become what we find him to be, it nevertheless associates itself only indirectly with the life we are living here and now.

No such objection as this, however, can be taken to our present subject; all readers of these lines have dreamed- probably many of them are in the habit of dreaming frequently; and they may therefore be interested in an endeavor to account for dream phenomena by the aid of the light thrown upon them by investigation along Theosophic lines.

The most convenient method in which we can arrange the various branches of our subject will perhaps be the following; first, to consider rather carefully the mechanism-physical, etheric and astral- by means of which impressions are conveyed to our consciousness; secondly, to see how the consciousness in its turn affects and uses this mechanism; thirdly, to note the condition both of the consciousness and its mechanism during sleep; and fourthly, to inquire how the various

4

DREAMS

kinds of dreams which men experience are thereby produced. As I am writing in the main for students of Theosophy, I shall feel myself at liberty to use, without detailed explanation, the ordinary Theosophical terms, with which I may safely assume them to be familiar, since otherwise my little book would far exceed its allotted limits. Should it, however, fall into the hands of any to whom the occasional use of such terms constitutes a difficulty, I can only apologize to them, and refer them for these preliminary explanations to any elementary Theosophical work, such as Mrs. Besant's Ancient Wisdom, ox Man and his Bodies.

DREAMS

CHAPTER II: THE MECHANISM

1. Physical

First, then, as to the physical part of the mechanism. We have in our bodies a great central axis of nervous matter, ending in the brain, and from this a network of nerve-threads radiates in every direction through the body. It is these nerve-threads, according to modern scientific theory, which by their vibrations convey all impressions from without to the brain, and the latter, upon receipt of these impressions, translates them into sensations or perceptions; so that if I put my hand upon some object and find it to be hot, it is really not my hand that feels, but my brain, which is acting upon information transmitted to it by the vibrations running along its telegraph wires, the nerve-threads. It is important also to bear in mind that all the nerve-threads of the body are the same in constitution, and that the special bundle of them that we call the optic nerve- which conveys to the brain impressions made upon the retina of the eye, and so enables us to see- differs from the nerve-threads of the hand or foot only in the fact that through long ages of evolution it has been specialized to receive and transmit most readily one particular small set of rapid vibrations which thus become visible to us as light. The same remark holds good with reference to our other sense organs; the auditory, the olfactory, or the gustatory nerves differ from one another and from the rest only in this specialization; they are essentially the same, and they all do their respective work in exactly the same manner, by the transmission of vibrations to the brain.

Now this brain of ours, which is thus the great center of our nervous system, is very readily affected by slight variations in our general health, and most especially by any which involve a change in the circulation of the blood through it. When the flow of blood through the vessels of the head is normal and regular, the brain (and, therefore, the whole nervous system) is at liberty to function in an orderly and efficient manner; but any alteration in this normal circulation, either as to quantity, quality, or speed, immediately produces a corresponding effect on the brain, and through it on the nerves throughout the body. If, for example, too much blood is supplied to the brain, congestion of the vessels takes place, and irregularity in its action is at once produced; if too little, the brain (and, therefore, the nervous system) becomes first irritable and then lethargic. The quality of the blood supplied is also of great importance.

As it courses through the body it has two principal functions to perform- to supply oxygen and to provide nutrition to the different organs of the body; and if it be unable adequately to fulfill either of these functions, a certain disorganization will follow. If the supply of oxygen to the brain be deficient, it becomes overcharged with carbon dioxide, and heaviness and lethargy very shortly supervene. A common example of this is the feeling of dullness and sleepiness which frequently overtakes one in a crowded and ill-ventilated room; owing to the exhaustion of the oxygen in the room by the continued respiration of so large a number of people, the brain does not receive its due modicum, and therefore is unable to do its work properly. Again, the speed with which the blood flows through the vessels affects the action of the brain; if it be too great, it produces fever; if too slow, then again lethargy is caused. It is obvious, therefore, that our brain (through which, be it remembered, all physical impressions must pass) may very easily be disturbed and more or less hindered in the due performance of its functions by causes apparently trivial- causes to which we should probably often pay no attention whatever, even during waking hours- of which we should almost certainly be entirely ignorant during sleep.

DREAMS

Before we pass on, one other peculiarity of this physical mechanism must be noted, and that is its remarkable tendency to repeat automatically vibrations to which it is accustomed to respond. It is to this property of the brain that are to be attributed all those bodily habits and tricks of manner which are entirely independent of the will, and are often so difficult to conquer; and, as will presently be seen, it plays an even more important part during sleep than it does in our waking life.

2. Etheric

It is not alone through the brain to which we have hitherto been referring, however, that impressions may be received by the man. Almost exactly coextensive with and interpenetrating his visible form is his etheric double (formerly called in Theosophical literature the linga sharira), and that also has a brain which is really no less physical than the other, though composed of matter in a condition finer than the gaseous. If we examine with psychic faculty the body of a newly-born child, we shall find it permeated not only by astral matter of every degree of density, but also by the different grades of etheric matter; and if we take the trouble to trace these inner bodies backwards to their origin, we find that it is of the latter that the etheric double-the mold upon which the physical body is built up- is formed by the agents of the Lords of karma; while the astral matter has been gathered together by the descending ego- not of course consciously, but automatically- as he passed through the astral plane, and is, in fact, merely the development in that plane of tendencies whose seeds have been lying dormant in him during his experiences in the heaven-world, because on that level it was impossible that they could germinate for want of the grade of matter necessary for their expression.

Now this etheric double has often been called the vehicle of the human life-ether or vital force (called in Sanskrit prana), and anyone who has developed the psychic faculties can see exactly how this is so. He will see the solar life-principle almost colorless, though intensely luminous and active, which is constantly poured into the earth's atmosphere by the sun; he will see how the etheric part of his spleen in the exercise of its wonderful function absorbs this universal life, and specializes it into prana, so that it may be more readily assimilable by his body; how it then courses all over that body, running along every nerve-thread in tiny globules of lovely rosy light, causing the glow of life and health and activity to penetrate every atom of the etheric double; and how, when the rose-colored particles have been absorbed, the superfluous life-ether finally radiates from the body in every direction as bluish-white light.

If he examines further into the action of this life-ether, he will soon see reason to believe that the transmission of impressions to the brain depends rather upon its regular flow along the etheric portion of the nerve-threads than upon the mere vibration of the particles of their denser and visible portion, as is commonly supposed. It would take too much of our space to detail all the experiments by which this theory is established, but the indication of one or two of the simplest will suffice to show the lines upon which they run. When a finger becomes entirely numbed with cold, it is incapable of feeling; and the same phenomenon of insensibility may readily be produced at will by a mesmerizer, who by a few passes over the arm of his subject will bring it into a condition in which it may be pricked with a needle or burnt by the flame of a candle without the slightest sensation of pain being experienced. Now why does the subject feel nothing in either of these two cases? The nerve threads are still there, and though in the first case it might be contended that their action was paralyzed by cold and by the absence of blood from the vessels, this certainly cannot be the reason in the second case, where the arm retains its normal temperature and the blood circulates as usual.

DREAMS

If we call in the aid of the clairvoyant, we shall be able to get somewhat nearer to a real explanation, for he will tell us that the reason why the frozen finger seems dead, and the blood is unable to circulate through its vessels, is because the rosy life-ether is no longer coursing along the nerve-threads; for we must remember that though matter in the etheric condition is invisible to ordinary sight, it is still purely physical, and, therefore, can be affected by the action of cold or heat. In the second case he will tell us that when the mesmerizer makes the passes by which he renders the subject's arm insensible, what he really does is to pour his own nerve-ether (or magnetism, as it is often called) into the arm, thereby driving back for the time that of the subject. The arm is still warm and living, because there is still life-ether coursing through it; but since it is no longer the subject's own specialized life-ether, and is therefore not en rapport with his brain, it conveys no information to that brain, and consequently there is no sense of feeling in the arm. From this it seems evident that though it is not absolutely the life-ether itself which does the work of conveying impressions from without to a man's brain, its presence as specialized by the man himself is certainly necessary for their due transmission along the nerve-threads.

Now just as any change in the circulation of the blood affects the receptivity of the denser brain matter, and thus modifies the reliability of the impressions derived through it, so the condition of the etheric portion of the brain is affected by any change in the volume or the velocity of these life currents. For example, when the quantity of nerve-ether specialized by the spleen falls for any reason below the average, physical weakness and weariness are immediately felt, and if, under these circumstances, it also happens that the speed of its circulation is increased, the man becomes super-sensitive, highly irritable, nervous, and perhaps even hysterical. While in such a condition he is often more sensitive to physical impressions than he would normally be, and so it often occurs that a person suffering from

10

ill health sees visions or apparitions which are imperceptible to his more robust neighbor. If, on the other hand, the volume and velocity of the life-ether are both reduced at the same time, the man experiences intense languor, becomes less sensitive to outside influences, and has a general feeling of being too weak to care much about what happens to him. It must be remembered also that the etheric matter of which we have spoken and the denser matter ordinarily recognized as belonging to the brain are really both parts of one and the same physical organism, and that, therefore, neither can be affected without instantly producing some reaction on the other. Consequently there can be no certainty that impressions will be correctly transmitted through this mechanism unless both portions of it are functioning quite normally; any irregularity in either part may very readily so dull or disturb its receptivity as to produce blurred or distorted images of whatever is presented to it. Furthermore, as will presently be explained, it is infinitely more liable to such aberrations during sleep than when in the waking state.

3. Astral

Still another mechanism that we have to take into account is the astral body, often called the desire-body. As its name implies, this vehicle is composed exclusively of astral matter, and is, in fact, the expression of the man on the astral plane, just as his physical body is the expression of him on the lower levels of the physical plane. Indeed, it will save the Theosophical student much trouble if he will learn to regard these different vehicles simply as the actual manifestation of the ego on their respective planes- if he understands, for example, that it is the causal body (sometimes called the auric egg) which is the real vehicle of the reincarnating ego, and is inhabited by him as long as he remains upon the plane which is his true home, the higher levels of the mental world; but that when he descends into the lower levels he must, in order to be able to function upon them, clothe himself in their matter, and that the matter which he thus attracts to himself furnishes his mind-body. Similarly, descending into the astral plane, he forms his astral or desire-body out of its matter, though, of course, still retaining all the other bodies; and on his still further descent to this lowest plane of all, the physical body is formed in the midst of the auric egg, which thus contains the entire man. This astral vehicle is even more sensitive to external impressions than the gross and etheric bodies, for it is itself the seat of all desires and emotions- the connecting link through which alone the ego can collect experiences from physical life. It is peculiarly susceptible to the influence of passing thought-currents, and when the mind is not actively controlling it, it is perpetually receiving these stimuli from without, and eagerly responding to them. This mechanism also, like the others, is more readily influenced during the sleep of the physical body. That this is so is shown by many observations, a fair example of them being a case recently reported to the writer, in which a man who had been a drunkard was describing the difficulties in the way of his reformation. He declared that after a long period of total abstinence he had succeeded in entirely destroying the physical desire for alcohol, so that in his waking condition he felt an absolute repulsion for it; yet he stated that he still frequently dreamed that he was drinking, and in that dream state he felt the old horrible pleasure in such degradation.

Apparently, therefore, during the day his desire was kept under control by the will, and casual thought-forms or passing elementals were unable to make any impression upon it; but when the astral body was liberated in sleep it escaped to some extent from the domination of the ego, and its extreme natural susceptibility so far reasserted itself that it again responded readily to these baneful influences, and imagined itself experiencing once more the disgraceful delights of detestable debauchery.

DREAMS

CHAPTER III: THE EGO

All these different portions of the mechanism are in reality merely instruments of the ego, though his control of them is as yet often very imperfect; for it must always be remembered that the ego is himself a developing entity, and that in the case of most of us he is scarcely more than a germ of what he is to be one day. A stanza in the Book of Dzyan tells us: "Those who received but a spark remained destitute of knowledge; the spark burned low"; and Madame Blavatsky explains that "those who received but a spark constitute the average humanity which have to acquire their intellectuality during the present manvantaric evolution." (Secret Doctrine, ii. 177.)

In the case of most of them that spark is still smoldering, and it will be many an age before its slow increase brings it to the stage of steady and brilliant flame. No doubt there are some passages in Theosophical literature which seem to imply that our higher ego needs no evolution, being already perfect and godlike on his own plane; but wherever such expressions are used, whatever may be the terminology employed, they must be taken to apply only to the atma, the true god within us, which is certainly far beyond the necessity of any kind of evolution of which we can know anything. The reincarnating ego most undoubtedly does evolve, and the process of his evolution can be very clearly seen by those who have developed clairvoyant vision to the extent necessary for the perception of that which exists on the higher levels of the mental plane. As before remarked, it is of the matter of that plane (if we may venture still to call it matter) that the comparatively permanent causal body, which he carries with him from birth to birth until the end of the human stage of his evolution, is composed. But though every individualized being must necessarily have such a body- since it is the possession of it which constitutes individualization- its

13

appearance is by no means similar in all cases. In fact, in the average unevolved man it is barely distinguishable at all, even by those who have the sight which unlocks for them the secrets of that plane, for it is a mere colorless film- just sufficient, apparently, to hold itself together and make a reincarnating individuality, but no more. (See Man Visible and Invisible, Plates V. and VIII.)

As soon, however, as the man begins to develop in spirituality, or even higher intellect, a change takes place. The real individual then begins to have a persisting character of his own, apart from that molded in each of his personalities in turn by training and surrounding circumstances; and this character shows itself in the size, color, luminosity, and definiteness of the causal body just as that of the personality shows itself in the mind-body, except that this higher vehicle is naturally subtler and more beautiful. (See ibid., Plate XXI.)

In one other respect, also, it happily differs from the bodies below it, and that is that in any ordinary circumstances no evil of any kind can manifest through it. The worst of men can commonly show himself on that plane only as an entirely undeveloped entity; his vices, even though continued through life after life, cannot soil that higher sheath; they can only make it more and more difficult to develop in it the opposite virtues.

On the other hand, perseverance along right lines soon tells upon the causal body, and in the case of a pupil who has made some progress on the Path of Holiness, it is a sight wonderful and lovely beyond all earthly conception (see ibid., Plate XXVI.); while that of an Adept is a magnificent sphere of living light, whose radiant glory no words can ever tell. He who has even once seen so sublime a spectacle as this, and can also see around him individuals at all stages of development between that and the colorless film of the ordinary person, can never feel any doubt as to the evolution of the reincarnating ego. The grasp which the ego has of his various instruments, and, therefore, his influence over them, is naturally small in his earlier stages. Neither his mind nor his passions are thoroughly under his control; indeed, the average man makes almost no effort to control them, but allows himself to be swept hither and thither just as his lower thoughts or desires suggest. Consequently, in sleep the different parts of the mechanism which we have mentioned are very apt to act almost entirely on their own account without reference to him, and the stage of his spiritual advancement is one of the factors that we have to take into account in considering the question of dreams. It is also important for us to realize the part which this ego takes in the formation of our conceptions of external objects. We must remember that what the vibrations of the nerve-threads present to the brain are merely impressions, and it is the work of the ego, acting through the mind, to classify, combine, and rearrange them.

For example, when I look out of the window and see a house and a tree, I instantly recognize them for what they are, yet the information really conveyed to me by my eyes falls very far short of such recognition. What actually happens is that certain rays of light that is, currents of ether vibrating at certain definite rates- are reflected from those objects and strike the retina of my eye, and the sensitive nerve-threads duly report those vibrations to the brain. But what is the tale they have to tell? All the information they really transmit is that in a particular direction there are certain varied patches of color bounded by more or less definite outlines. It is the mind which from its past experience is able to decide that one particular square white object is a house, and another rounded green one is a tree, and that they are both probably of such and such a size, and at such and such a distance from me.

DREAMS

A person who, having been born blind, obtains his sight by means of an operation, does not for some time know what are the objects he sees, nor can he judge their distance from him. The same is true of a baby, for it may often be seen grasping at attractive objects (such as the moon, for example) which are far out of its reach; but as it grows up it unconsciously learns, by repeated experience, to judge instinctively the probable distance and size of the form it sees. Yet even grown-up people may very readily be deceived as to the distance, and therefore the size, of any unfamiliar object, especially if seen in a dim or uncertain light. We see, therefore, that mere vision is by no means sufficient for accurate perception, but that the discrimination of the ego acting through the mind must be brought to bear upon what is seen; and furthermore, we see that this discrimination is not an inherent instinct of the mind, perfect from the first, but is the result of the unconscious comparison of a number of experiences- points which must be carefully borne in mind when we come to the next division of our subject.

DREAMS

CHAPTER IV: THE CONDITION OF SLEEP

Clairvoyant observation bears abundant testimony to the fact that when a man falls into deep slumber the higher principles in their astral vehicle almost invariably withdraw from the body, and hover in its immediate neighborhood. Indeed, it is the process of this withdrawal which we commonly call "going to sleep." In considering the phenomena of dreams, therefore, we have to bear in mind this re-arrangement, and see how it affects both the ego and his various mechanisms. In the case we are to examine, then, we assume that our subject is in deep sleep, the physical body (including that finer portion of it which is often called the etheric double) lying quietly on the bed, while the ego, in its astral body, floats with equal tranquility just above it. What, under these circumstances, will be the condition and the consciousness of these several principles?

1. The Brain

When the ego has thus for the time resigned the control of his brain, it does not therefore become entirely unconscious, as one would perhaps expect. It is evident from various experiments that the physical body has a certain dim consciousness of its own, quite apart from that of the real self, and apart also from the mere aggregate of the consciousness of its individual cells.

The writer has several times observed an effect of this consciousness when watching the extraction of a tooth under the influence of gas. The body uttered a confused cry, and raised its hands vaguely towards the mouth, clearly showing that it to some extent felt the wrench; yet when the ego resumed possession twenty seconds later, he declared that he had felt absolutely nothing of the operation. Of course I am aware that such movements are ordinarily attributed to "reflex action," and that people are in the habit of accepting that statement as though it were a real explanation- not seeing that as employed here it is a mere phrase, and explains nothing whatever.

This consciousness then, such as it is, is still working in the physical brain although the ego floats above it, but its grasp is, of course, far feebler than that of the man himself, and consequently all those causes which were mentioned above as likely to affect the action of the brain are now capable of influencing it to a very much greater extent. The slightest alteration in the supply or circulation of the blood now produces grave irregularities of action, and this is why indigestion, as affecting the flow of the blood, so frequently causes troubled sleep or bad dreams. But even when undisturbed, this strange, dim consciousness has many remarkable peculiarities. Its action seems to be to a great extent automatic, and the results are usually incoherent, senseless, and hopelessly confused. It seems unable to apprehend an idea except in the form of a scene in which it is itself an actor, and therefore all stimuli, whether from within or without, are forthwith translated into perceptual images. It is incapable of grasping abstract ideas or memories as such; they immediately become imaginary precepts. If, for example, the idea of glory could be suggested to that consciousness, it could take shape only as a vision of some glorious being appearing before the dreamer; if a thought of hatred somehow came across it, it could be appreciated only as a scene in which some imaginary actor showed violent hatred towards the sleeper.

Again, every local direction of thought becomes for it an absolute spacial transportation. If during our waking hours we think of China or Japan, our thought is at once, as it were, in those countries; but nevertheless we are perfectly aware that our physical bodies are exactly where they were a moment before. In the condition of consciousness which we are considering, however, there is no discriminating ego to balance the cruder impressions, and consequently any passing thought suggesting China and Japan could image itself only as an actual, instantaneous transportation to those countries, and the dreamer would suddenly find himself there, surrounded by as much of the appropriate circumstance as he happened to be able to remember. It has often been noted that while startling transitions of this sort are extremely frequent in dreams, the sleeper never seems at the time to feel any surprise at their suddenness. This phenomenon is easily explicable when examined by the light of such observations as we are considering, for in the mere consciousness of the physical brain there is nothing capable of such a feeling as surprise- it simply perceives the pictures as they appear before it; it has no power to judge either of their sequence or their lack of that quality. Another source of the extraordinary confusion visible in this half-consciousness is the manner in which the law of the association of ideas works in it. We are all familiar with the wonderful instantaneous action of this law in waking life; we know how a chance word- a strain of music- even the scent- of a flower- may be sufficient to bring back to the mind a chain of long-forgotten memories. Now in the sleeping brain this law is as active as ever, but it acts under curious limitations; every such association of ideas, whether abstract or concrete, becomes a mere combination of images; and as our association of ideas is often merely by synchronism, as of events which, though really entirely unconnected, happened to us in succession, it may readily be imagined that the most inextricable confusion of these images is of frequent occurrence, while their number is practically infinite, as whatever can be dragged from the immense stores of memory appears in pictorial form.

Naturally enough a succession of such pictures is rarely perfectly recoverable by memory, since there is no order to help in recovery- just as it may be easy enough to remember in waking life a connected sentence or a verse of poetry, even when heard only once, whereas without some system of mnemonics it would be almost impossible to recollect accurately a mere jumble of meaningless words under similar circumstances. Another peculiarity of this curious consciousness of the brain is, that while singularly sensitive to the slightest external influences, such as sounds or touches, it yet magnifies and distorts them to an almost incredible degree. All writers on dreams give examples of this, and, indeed, some will probably be within the knowledge of every one who has paid any attention to the subject.

Among the stories most commonly told is one of a man who had a painful dream of being hanged because his shirt-collar was too tight; another man magnified the prick of a pin into a fatal stab received in a duel; another translated a slight pinch into the bite of a wild beast. Maury relates that part of the rail at the head of his bed once became detached and fell across his neck, so as just to touch it lightly; yet this trifling contact produced a terrible dream of the French Revolution, in which he seemed to himself to perish by the guillotine.

Another writer tells us that he frequently awakened from sleep with a confused remembrance of dreams full of noise, of loud voices and thunderous sounds, and was entirely unable for a long time to discover their origin; but at last he succeeded in tracing them to the murmurous sound made in the ear (perhaps by the circulation of the blood) when it is laid on the pillow, much as a similar but louder murmur may be heard by holding a shell to the ear.

It must by this time be evident that even from this bodily brain alone there comes enough confusion and exaggeration to account for many of the dream phenomena; but this is only one of the factors that we have to take into consideration.

DREAMS

2. The Etheric Brain

It will be obvious that this part of the organism, so sensitive to every influence even during our waking life, must be still more susceptible when in the condition of sleep. When examined under these circumstances by a clairvoyant, streams of thought are seen to be constantly sweeping through it- not its own thoughts in the least, for it has of itself no power to think- but the casual thoughts of others which are always floating round us. Students of occultism are well aware that it is indeed true that "thoughts are things," for every thought impresses itself upon the plastic elemental essence, and generates a temporary living entity, the duration of whose life depends upon the energy of the thought-impulse given to it. We are therefore living in the midst of an ocean of other men's thoughts, and whether we are awake or asleep, these are constantly presenting themselves to the etheric part of our brain. So long as we ourselves are actively thinking, and therefore keeping our brain fully employed, it is practically impervious to this continual impingement of thought from without; but the moment that we leave it idle, the stream of inconsequential chaos begins to pour through it. Most of the thoughts sweep through unassimilated and almost unnoticed, but now and then one comes along which reawakens some vibrations to which the etheric part of the brain is accustomed; at once that brain seizes upon it, intensifies it, and makes it its own; that thought in turn suggests another, and so a whole train of ideas is started, until eventually it also fades away, and the disconnected, purposeless stream begins flowing through the brain again.

The vast majority of people, if they will watch what they are in the habit of calling their thoughts closely, will find that they are very largely made up of a casual stream of this sort- that in truth they are not their thoughts at all, but simply the cast-off fragments of other people's. For the ordinary man seems to have no control whatever over his mind; he hardly ever knows exactly of what he is thinking at any particular moment, or why he is thinking of it, instead of directing his mind to some definite point, he allows it to run riot at its own sweet will, or lets it lie fallow, so that any casual seed cast into it by the wind may germinate and come to fruition there.

The result of this is that even when he, the ego, really wishes for once to think consecutively on any particular subject, he finds himself practically unable to do so; all sorts of stray thoughts rush in unbidden from every side, and since he is quite unused to controlling his mind, he is powerless to stem the torrent. Such a person does not know what real concentrated thought is; and it is this utter lack of concentration, this feebleness of mind and will, that makes the early stages of occult development so difficult to the average man. Again, since in the present state of the world's evolution there are likely to be more evil thoughts than good ones floating around him, this weakness lays him open to all sorts of temptations which a little care and effort might have avoided altogether. In sleep, then, the etheric part of the brain is even more than usually at the mercy of these thought currents, since the ego is, for the time, in less close association with it. A curious fact brought out in some recent experiments is that when by any means these currents are shut out from this part of the brain, it does not remain absolutely passive, but begins very slowly and dreamily to evolve pictures for itself from its store of past memories. An example of this will be given later, when some of these experiments are described.

3. The Astral Body

As before mentioned, it is in this vehicle that the ego is functioning during sleep, and it is usually to be seen (by anyone whose inner sight is opened) hovering over the physical body on the bed. Its appearance, however, differs very greatly according to the stage of development which the ego to which it belongs has reached. In the case of the entirely uncultured and undeveloped person it is simply a floating wreath of mist, roughly ovoid in shape, but very irregular and indefinite in outline, while the figure within the mist (the denser astral counterpart of the physical body) is also vague, though generally recognizable.

It is receptive only of the coarser and more violent vibrations of desire, and unable to move more than a few yards away from its physical body; but as evolution progresses, the ovoid mist becomes more and more definite in outline, and the figure within it more and more nearly a perfect image of the physical body beneath it. Its receptivity simultaneously increases, until it is instantly responsive to all the vibrations of its plane, the finer as well as the more ignoble; though in the astral body of a highly-developed person there would naturally be practically no matter left coarse enough to respond to the latter. Its power of locomotion also becomes much greater; it can travel without discomfort to considerable distances from its physical encasement, and can bring back more or less definite impressions as to places which it may have visited and people whom it may have met. In every case this astral body is, as ever, intensely impressionable by any thought or suggestion involving desire, though in some the desires which most readily awaken a response in it may be somewhat higher than in others.

4. The Ego in Sleep

Though the condition in which the astral body is to be found during sleep changes largely as evolution takes place, that of the ego inhabiting it changes still more. Where the former is in the stage of the floating wreath of mist, the ego is practically almost as much asleep as the body lying below him; he is blind to the sights and deaf to the voices of his own higher plane, and even if some idea belonging to it should by chance reach him, since he has no control over his mechanism, he will be quite unable to impress it upon his physical brain so that it may be remembered upon waking.

If a man in this primitive condition recollects anything at all of what happens to him during sleep, it will almost invariably be the result of purely physical impressions made upon the brain either from within or from without- any experience which his real ego may have had being forgotten. Sleepers may be observed at all stages from this condition of all but blank oblivion, up to full and perfect consciousness on the astral plane, though this latter is naturally comparatively rare. Even a man who is sufficiently awake to meet not infrequently with important experiences in this higher life, may yet be (and often is) unable so far to dominate his brain as to check its current of inconsequential thought pictures and impress upon it instead what he wishes it to recollect; and thus when his physical body awakes he may have only the most confused memory, or no memory at all, of what has really happened to him. And this is a pity, for he may meet with much that is of the greatest interest and importance to him.

Not only may he visit distant scenes of surpassing beauty, but he may meet and exchange ideas with friends, either living or departed, who happen^to be equally awake on the astral plane. He may be fortunate enough to encounter those who know far more than he does, and may receive warning or instruction from them ; he may, on the other hand, be privileged to help and comfort some who know less than himself. He may come into contact with non-human entities of various kinds- with nature spirits, artificial elementals, or even, though very rarely, with Devas; he will be subject to all kinds of influences, good or evil, strengthening or terrifying.

24

DREAMS

HIS TRANSCENDENTAL MEASURE OF TIME

But whether he remembers anything when physically awake or not, the ego who is fully or even partially conscious of his surroundings on the astral plane is beginning to enter into his heritage of powers, which far transcend those he possesses down here; for his consciousness when thus liberated from the physical body has very remarkable possibilities. His measure of time and space is so entirely different from that which we use in waking life, that from our view it seems as though neither time nor space existed for him. I do not wish here to discuss the question, intensely interesting though it be, as to whether time can be said really to exist, or whether it is but a limitation of this lower consciousness, and all that we call time- past, present and future alike- is "but one eternal Now"; I wish only to show that when the ego is freed from physical trammels, either during sleep, trance or death, he appears to employ some transcendental measure of time which has nothing in common with our ordinary physiological one.

A hundred stories might be told to prove this fact; it will be sufficient if I give two- the first a very old one (related, I think, by Addison in The Spectator), the other an account of an event which happened but a short time ago, and has never before appeared in print.

ILLUSTRATIVE EXAMPLES OF IT

It seems that in the Koran there is a wonderful narrative concerning a visit paid one morning by the prophet Muhammad to heaven, during which he saw many different regions there, had them all very fully explained to him, and also had numerous lengthy conferences with various angels; yet when he returned to his body, the bed from which he had risen was still warm, and he found that but a few seconds had passed- in fact, I believe the water had not yet all run out from a jug which he had accidentally overturned as he started on the expedition!

Now Addison's story runs that a certain sultan of Egypt felt it impossible to believe this, and even went to the impolitic length of bluntly declaring to his religious teacher that the tale was a falsehood. The teacher, who was a great doctor learned in the law, and credited with miraculous powers, undertook to prove on the spot to the doubting monarch that the story was, at any rate, not impossible. He had a large basin of water brought, and begged the sultan just to dip his head into the water and withdraw it as quickly as he could.

The king accordingly plunged his head into the basin, and to his intense surprise found himself at once in a place entirely unknown to him- on a lonely shore, near the foot of a great mountain. After the first stupefaction was over, what was probably the most natural idea for an oriental monarch came into his head- he thought he was bewitched, and at once began to execrate the doctor for such abominable treachery. However, time passed on; he began to get hungry, and realized that there was nothing for it but to find some means of livelihood in this strange country. After wandering about for some time, he found some men at work felling trees in a wood, and applied to them for assistance. They set him to help them, and eventually took him with them to the town where they lived. Here he resided and worked for some years, gradually amassing money, and at length contrived to marry a rich wife. With her he spent many happy years of wedded life, bringing up a family of no less than fourteen children, but after her death he met with so many misfortunes that he at last fell into want again, and once more, in his old age, became a wood-porter.

One day, walking by the seaside, he threw off his clothes

and plunged into the sea for a bath; and as he raised his head and shook the water from his eyes, he was astounded to find himself standing among his old courtiers, with his teacher of long ago at his side, and a basin of water before him.

It was long- and no wonder- before he could be brought to believe that all those years of incident and adventure had been nothing but one moment's dream, caused by the hypnotic suggestion of his teacher, and that really he had done nothing but dip his head quickly into the basin of water and draw it out again. This is a good story, and illustrates our point well, but, of course, we have no proof whatever as to its truth. It is quite different, however, with regard to an event that happened only the other day to a well-known man of science. He unfortunately had to have two teeth removed, and took gas in the ordinary way for that purpose. Being interested in such problems as these, he had resolved to note very carefully his sensations all through the operation, but as he inhaled the gas, such a drowsy contentment stole over him that he soon forgot his intention, and seemed to sink into sleep.

He rose next morning, as he supposed, and went on with his regular round of scientific experiment, lecturing before various learned bodies, etc., but all with a singular sense of enhanced power and pleasure- every lecture being a remarkable achievement, every experiment leading to new and magnificent discoveries. This went on day after day, week after week, for a very considerable period, though the exact time is uncertain; until at last one day, when he was delivering a lecture before the Royal Society, he was annoyed by the unmannerly behavior of some one present, who disturbed him by remarking, "It's all over now"; and as he turned round to see what this meant, another voice observed, "They are both out." Then he realized that he was still sitting in the dentist's chair, and that he had lived through that period of intensified life in just forty seconds!

DREAMS

Neither of these cases, it may be said, was exactly an ordinary dream. But the same thing occurs constantly in ordinary dreams, and there is again abundant testimony to show it. Steffens, one of the German writers on the subject, relates how when a boy he was sleeping with his brother, and dreamed that he was in a lonely street, pursued by some dreadful wild beast. He ran on in great terror, though unable to cry out, until he came to a staircase, up which he turned, but being exhausted with fright and hard running, was overtaken by the animal, and severely bitten in the thigh. He awoke with a start, and found that his brother had pinched him on the thigh.

Richers, another German writer, tells the story of a man who was awakened by the firing of a shot, which yet came in as the conclusion of a long dream, in which he had become a soldier, had deserted and suffered terrible hardships, had been captured, tried, condemned, and finally shot- the whole long drama being lived through in the moment of being awakened by the sound of the shot. Again, we have the tale of the man who fell asleep in an armchair while smoking a cigar, and after dreaming through an eventful life of many years, awoke to find his cigar still alight. One might multiply authenticated cases to any extent.

HIS POWER OF DRAMATIZATION

Another remarkable peculiarity of the ego, in addition to his transcendental measure of time, is suggested by some of these stories, and that is his faculty, or, perhaps, we should rather say his habit, of instantaneous dramatization. It will be noticed in the cases of the shot and the pinch which have just been narrated, that the physical effect which awakened the person came as the climax to a dream apparently extending over a considerable space of time, though obviously suggested in reality entirely by that physical effect itself.

DREAMS

Now the news, so to speak, of this physical effect, whether it be a sound or a touch, has to be conveyed to the brain by the nerve-threads, and this transmission takes a certain space of time- only a minute fraction of a second, of course, but still a definite amount which is calculable and measurable by the exceedingly delicate instruments used in modern scientific research. The ego, when out of the body, is able to perceive in an absolutely instantaneous manner without the use of the nerves, and consequently is aware of what happens just that minute fraction of a second before the information reaches his physical brain.

In that barely-appreciable space of time he appears to compose a kind of drama or series of scenes, leading up to and culminating in the event which awakens the physical body; and when after waking he is limited by the organs of that body, he becomes incapable of distinguishing in memory between the subjective and the objective, and therefore imagines himself to have really acted through his own drama in a dream state. This habit, however, seems to be peculiar to the ego which, as far as spirituality goes, is still comparatively undeveloped; as evolution takes place, and the real man slowly comes to understand his position and his responsibilities, he rises beyond these graceful sports of his childhood. It would seem that just as primitive man casts every natural phenomenon into the form of a myth, so the unadvanced ego dramatizes every event that comes under his notice; but the man who has attained continuous consciousness finds himself so fully occupied in the work of the higher planes that he devotes no energy to such matters, and therefore he dreams no more.

HIS FACULTY OF PREVISION

Another result which follows from the ego's supernormal method of time-measurement is that in some degree prevision is possible to him. The present, the past, and, to a certain extent, the future lie open before him if he knows how to read them; and he undoubtedly thus foresees at times events that will be of interest or importance to his lower personality, and makes more or less successful endeavors to impress them upon it. When we take into account the stupendous difficulties in his way in the case of an ordinary person- the fact that he is himself probably not yet even half awake, that he has hardly any control over his various vehicles, and cannot, therefore, prevent his message from being distorted or altogether overpowered by the surgings of desire, by the casual thought-currents in the etheric part of his brain, or by some slight physical disturbance affecting his denser body- we shall not wonder that he so rarely fully succeeds in his attempt. Once, now and again, a complete and perfect forecast of some event is vividly brought back from the realms of sleep; far more often the picture is distorted or unrecognizable, while sometimes all that comes through is a vague sense of some impending misfortune, and still more frequently nothing at all penetrates the denser body.

It has sometimes been argued that when this prevision occurs it must be mere coincidence, since if events could really be foreseen they must be fore-ordained, in which case there can be no free-will for man. Man, however, undoubtedly does possess free-will; and therefore, as remarked above, prevision is possible only to a certain extent. In the affairs of the average man it is probably possible to a very large extent, since he has developed no will of his own worth speaking of, and is consequently very largely the creature of circumstances; his karma places him amid certain surroundings, and their action upon him is so much the most important factor in his history that his future course may be foreseen with almost mathematical certainty.

When we consider the vast number of events which can

be but little affected by human action, and also the complex and wide-spreading relation of causes to their effects, it will scarcely seem wonderful to us that on the plane where the result of all causes at present in action is visible, a very large portion of the future may be foretold with considerable accuracy even as to detail. That this can be done has been proved again and again, not only by prophetic dreams, but by the second-sight of the Highlanders and the predictions of clairvoyants, and it is on this forecasting of effects from the causes already in existence that the whole scheme of astrology is based. But when we come to deal with a developed individual- a man with knowledge and will- then prophecy fails us, for he is no longer the creature of circumstances, but to a great extent their master.

True, the main events of his life are arranged beforehand by his past karma; but the way in which he will allow them to affect him, the method by which he will deal with them, and perhaps triumph over them- these are his own, and they cannot be foreseen except as probabilities. Such actions of his in their turn become causes, and thus chains of effects are produced in his life which were not provided for by the original arrangement, and, therefore, could not have been foretold with any exactitude. An analogy may be taken from a simple experiment in mechanics; if a certain amount of force be employed to set a ball rolling, we cannot in any way destroy or decrease that force when once the ball has started, but we can counteract or modify its actions by the application of a fresh force in a different direction. An equal force applied to the ball in exactly the opposite direction will stop it entirely; a lesser force so applied will reduce its speed, any force applied from either side will alter both its speed and its direction. So with the working out of destiny. It is clear that at any given moment a body of causes is in action which, if not interfered with, will inevitably produce certain results- results which on higher planes would seem already present, and could therefore be exactly described; but it is also clear that a man of strong will can, by setting up new forces, largely modify these results; and these modifications could not be foreseen by any ordinary clairvoyance until after the new forces had been set in motion.

EXAMPLES OF ITS USE

Two incidents which recently came to the knowledge of the writer will serve as excellent illustrations both of the possibility of prevision and also of its modification by a determined will. A gentleman whose hand is often used for automatic writing one day received in that way a communication professing to come from a person whom he knew slightly, in which she informed him that she was in a great state of indignation and annoyance because, having arranged to give a certain lecture, she found no one in the hall at the appointed time, and was consequently unable to deliver her discourse. Meeting the lady in question a few days later, and supposing the letter to refer to a past event, he condoled with her on the disappointment, and she remarked with great surprise that what he told her was certainly very odd, as, though she had not yet delivered her lecture, she was to do so the following week, and she hoped the letter might not prove a prophecy. Unlikely as such an event seemed, the account written did prove to be a prophecy; no one attended at the hall, the lecture was not delivered, and the lecturer was much annoyed and distressed, exactly as the automatic writing had foretold. What kind of entity inspired the writing does not appear, but it was evidently one who moved on a plane where prevision was possible; and it may really have been, as it professed to be, the ego of the lecturer, anxious to break the disappointment to her by preparing her mind for it on this lower plane.

If it were so, it will be said, why should he not have influenced her directly? He may very well have been quite unable to do this, and the sensitivity of her friend may have been the only possible channel through which he could convey his warning. Roundabout as this method may seem, students of these subjects are well aware that there are many examples in which it is evident that means of communication such as are here employed are absolutely the only ones available. On another occasion the same gentleman received in the same way what purported to be a letter from another feminine friend, relating a long and sad story from her recent life. She explained that she was in very great trouble, and that all the difficulty had originally arisen from a conversation (which she gave in detail) with a certain person, by means of which she was persuaded, much against her own feeling, to adopt a particular course of action. She went on to describe how, a year or so later, a series of events directly attributable to her adoption of this course of action ensued, culminating in the commission of a horrible crime, which had for ever darkened her life. As in the previous case, when next the gentleman met the friend from whom the letter was supposed to come, he told her what it had contained. She knew nothing whatever of any such story, and though she was greatly impressed by its circumstantiality, they eventually decided that there was nothing in it. Some time later, to her intense surprise, the conversation foretold in the letter actually took place, and she found herself being implored to take the very course of action to which so disastrous an ending had been foreshadowed. She would certainly have yielded, distrusting her own judgment, but for the memory of the prophecy; having that in mind, however, she resisted in the most determined manner, even though her attitude caused surprise and pain to the friend with whom she was talking. The course of action indicated in the letter not being followed, the time of the predicted catastrophe naturally arrived and passed without any unusual incident. So it might have done in any case, it may be said. Perhaps so; and yet, remembering how exactly that other prediction was fulfilled, one cannot but feel that the warning conveyed by this writing probably prevented the commission of a crime. If that be so, then here is a good example of the way in which our future may be altered by the exercise of a determined will.

HIS SYMBOLIC THOUGHT

Another point worth notice in relation to the condition of the ego when out of the body during sleep is that he appears to think in symbols- that is to say, that what down here would be an idea requiring many words to express, is perfectly conveyed to him by a single symbolical image. Now when such a thought as this is impressed upon the brain, and so remembered in the waking consciousness, it of course needs translation. Often the mind duly performs this function, but sometimes the symbol is recollected without its key- comes through untranslated, as it were; and then confusion arises. Many people, however, are quite in the habit of bringing the symbols through in this manner, and trying to invent an interpretation down here. In such cases, each person seems usually to have a system of symbology of his own. Mrs. Crowe mentions, in her Night Side of Nature (p. 54), "a lady who, whenever a misfortune was impending, dreamed that she saw a large fish. One night she dreamed that this fish had bitten two of her little boy's fingers. Immediately afterwards a school-fellow of the child's injured those two very fingers by striking him with a hatchet. I have met with several persons who have learned by experience to consider one particular dream as the certain prognostic of misfortune." There are, however, a few points upon which most of these dreamers agree- as, for example, that to dream of deep water signifies approaching trouble, and that pearls are a sign of tears.

5. The Factors in the Production of Dreams

Having thus examined the condition of man during sleep, we see that the factors which may be concerned in the

DREAMS

production of dreams are:

1. The ego, who may be in any state of consciousness from almost utter insensibility to perfect command of his faculties, and as he approximates to the latter condition, enters more and more fully into possession of certain powers transcending any that most of us possess in our ordinary waking state.

2. The astral body, ever palpitating with the wild surgings of emotion and desire.

3. The etheric part of the brain, with a ceaseless procession of disconnected pictures sweeping through it.

4. The lower physical brain, with its infantile semi-consciousness and its habit of expressing every stimulus in pictorial form.

When we go to sleep our ego withdraws further within himself, and leaves his various encasements freer to go their own way than they usually are; but it must be remembered that the separate consciousness of these vehicles, when they are thus allowed to show it, is of a very rudimentary character. When we add that each of these factors is then infinitely more susceptible of impression from without even than it ordinarily is, we shall see small cause to wonder that the recollection on waking, which is a sort of synthesis of all the different activities which have been going on, should generally be somewhat confused. Let us now, with these thoughts in our minds, see how the different kinds of dreams usually experienced are to be accounted for.

CHAPTER V: DREAMS

1. The True Vision

This, which cannot properly be classified as a dream at all, is a case where the ego either sees for himself some fact upon a higher plane of nature, or else has it impressed upon him by a more advanced entity; at any rate he is made aware of some fact which it is important for him to know, or perhaps sees some glorious and ennobling vision which encourages and strengthens him. Happy is the man to whom such vision comes with sufficient clearness to make its way through all obstacles and fix itself firmly in his waking memory.

2. The Prophetic Dream

This also we must attribute exclusively to the action of the ego, who either foresees for himself or is told of some future event for which he wishes to prepare his lower consciousness. This may be of any degree of clearness and accuracy, according to the power of the ego to assimilate it himself, and, having done so, to impress it upon his waking brain. Sometimes the event is one of serious moment, such as death or disaster, so that the motive of the ego in endeavoring to impress it is obvious. On other occasions, however, the fact foretold is apparently unimportant, and it is difficult for us to comprehend why the ego should take any trouble about it. Of course it is always possible that in such a case the fact remembered may be only a trifling detail of some far larger vision, the rest of which has not come through to the physical brain.

Often the prophecy is evidently intended as a warning, and instances are not wanting in which that warning has been taken, and so the dreamer has been saved from injury or death. In most cases the hint is neglected, or its true signification not understood until the fulfillment comes. In others an attempt is made to act upon the suggestion, but, nevertheless, circumstances over which the dreamer has no control bring him in spite of himself into the position foretold. Stories of such prophetic dreams are so common that the reader may easily find some in almost any of the books on such subjects. I quote a recent example from Mr. W. T. Stead's Real Ghost Stones (p. 77) The hero of the tale was a blacksmith at a manufacturing mill, which was driven by a water-wheel. He knew the wheel to be out of repair, and one night he dreamed that at the close of the next day's work the manager detained him to repair it, that his foot slipped and became entangled between the two wheels, and was injured and afterwards amputated. He told his wife the dream in the morning, and made up his mind to be out of the way that evening, if he was wanted to repair the wheel.

During the day the manager announced that the wheel must be repaired when the work people left that evening, but the blacksmith determined to make himself scarce before the hour arrived. He fled to a wood in the vicinity, and thought to hide himself there in its recesses. He came to a spot where lay some timber which belonged to the mill, and detected a lad stealing some pieces of wood from the heap. On this he pursued him in order to rescue the stolen property, and became so excited that he forgot all about his resolution, and ere he was aware of it, found himself back at the mill just as the workmen were being dismissed. He could not escape notice, and as he was principal smith, he had to go upon the wheel, but he resolved to be unusually careful. In spite of all his care, however, his foot slipped and got entangled between the two wheels, just as he had dreamed. It was crushed so badly that he had to be carried to the Bradford Infirmary, where the leg was amputated above the knee; so the prophetic dream was fulfilled throughout.

DREAMS

3. The Symbolical Dream

This, too, is the work of the ego, and, indeed, it might almost be defined as a less successful variant of the preceding class, for it is, after all, an imperfectly translated effort on his part to convey information as to the future. A good example of this kind of dream was described by Sir Noel Paton in a letter to Mrs. Crowe, published by the latter in The Night Side of Nature (p. 54). The great artist writes:

"That dream of my mother's was as follows. She stood in a long, dark, empty gallery; on one side was my father, on the other my eldest sister, then myself and the rest of the family according to their ages We all stood silent and motionless. At last it entered- the unimagined something that, casting its grim shadow before, had enveloped all the trivialities of the preceding dream in the stifling atmosphere of terror. It entered, stealthily descending the three steps that led from the entrance down into the chamber of horror; and my mother felt that it was Death. He carried on his shoulder a heavy ax, and had come, she thought, to destroy all her little ones at one fell swoop. On the entrance of the shape my sister Alexes leaped out of the rank, interposing herself between him and my mother. He raised his ax and aimed a blow at my sister Catherine- a blow which, to her horror, my mother could not intercept, though she had snatched up a three-legged stool for that purpose. She could not, she felt, fling the stool at the figure without destroying Alexes, who kept shooting out and in between her and the ghastly thing Down came the ax, and poor Catherine fell... Again the ax was lifted by the inexorable shape over the head of my brother, who stood next in the line, but now Alexes had disappeared somewhere behind the ghastly visitant, and with a scream my mother flung the stool at his head. He vanished and she awoke. Three months had elapsed, when we children were all of us seized with scarlet fever. My

38

sister Catherine died almost immediately- sacrificed, as my mother in her misery thought, to her (my mother's) over-anxiety for Alexes, whose danger seemed more imminent. The dream prophecy was in part fulfilled. I also was at death's door- given up by the doctors, but not by my mother; she was confident of my recovery. But for my brother, who was scarcely considered in danger at all, but over whose head she had seen the visionary ax impending, her fears were great: for she could not recollect whether the blow had or had not descended when the specter vanished. My brother recovered, but relapsed, and barely escaped with life; but Alexes did not. For a year and ten months the poor child lingered... and I held her little hand as she died Thus the dream was fulfilled."

It is very curious to notice here how accurately the details of the symbolism work themselves out, even to the supposed sacrifice of Catherine for the sake of Alexes, and the difference in the manner of their deaths.

4. The Vivid and Connected Dream

This is sometimes a remembrance, more or less accurate, of a real astral experience which has occurred to the ego while wandering away from his sleeping physical body; more frequently, perhaps, it is the dramatization by that ego either of the impression produced by some trifling physical sound or touch, or of some casual idea which happens to strike him. Examples of this latter kind have already been given, and there are many to be found of the former also. We may take as an instance an anecdote quoted by Mr. Andrew Lang, in Dreams and Ghosts (p. 35), from the distinguished French physician Dr. Brierre de Boismont, who describes it as occurring within his own intimate knowledge.

"Miss C., a lady of excellent sense, lived before her

marriage in the house of her uncle D., a celebrated physician and member of the Institute. Her mother at this time was seriously ill in the country. One night the girl dreamed that she saw her mother, pale and dying, and especially grieved at the absence of two of her children- one a cure in Spain, and the other (herself) in Paris. Next she heard her own Christian name called, 'Charlotte!' and in her dream saw the people about her mother bring in her own little niece and godchild Charlotte from the next room. The patient intimated by a sign that she did not want this Charlotte, but her daughter in Paris. She displayed the deepest regret; her countenance changed, she fell back and died. Next day the melancholy of Miss C. attracted the attention of her uncle. She told him her dream, and he admitted that her mother was dead. Some months later, when her uncle was absent, she arranged his papers, which he did not like anyone to touch. Among these was a letter containing the story of her mother's death, and giving all the details of her own dream, which D. had kept concealed lest they should impress her too painfully."

Sometimes the clairvoyant dream refers to a matter of much less importance than a death, as in the following case, which is given by Dr. F. G. Lee in Glimpses in the Twilight (p. 108). A mother dreams that she sees her son on a boat of strange shape, standing at the foot of a ladder which leads to an upper deck. He looks extremely pale and worn, and says to her earnestly, "Mother, I have nowhere to sleep." In due course a letter arrives from the son, in which he encloses a sketch of the curious boat, showing the ladder leading to the upper deck; he also explained that on a certain day (that of his mother's dream) a storm nearly wrecked their boat and hopelessly soaked his bed, and the account ends with the words, " I had nowhere to sleep."

It is quite clear that in both these cases the dreamers, drawn by thoughts of love or anxiety, had really traveled in the astral body during sleep to those in whose fate they were so keenly interested, and simply witnessed the various occurrences as they took place.

5. The Confused Dream

This, which is by far the commonest of all, may be caused, as has already been pointed out, in various ways. It may be simply a more or less perfect recollection of a series of the disconnected pictures and impossible transformations produced by the senseless automatic action of the lower physical brain; it may be a reproduction of the stream of casual thought which has been pouring through the etheric part of the brain; if sensual images of any kind enter into it, it is due to the ever-restless tide of earthly desire, probably stimulated by some unholy influence of the astral world; it may be due to an imperfect attempt at dramatization on the part of an undeveloped ego, or it may be (and most often is) due to an inextricable mingling of several or all of these influences. The way in which such mingling takes place will perhaps be made clearer by a short account of some of the experiments on the dream state recently made by the London Lodge of the Theosophical Society, with the aid of some clairvoyant investigators among its members.

DREAMS

CHAPTER VI: EXPERIMENTS ON THE DREAM-STATE

The object specially in view in the investigation, part of which I am about to describe, was to discover whether it was possible to impress the ego of an ordinary person during sleep sufficiently to enable him to recollect the circumstance when he awoke; and it was also desired, as far as possible, to find out what are the obstacles that usually stand in the way of such recollection. The first experiment tried was with an average man of small education and rough exterior- a man of the Australian shepherd type- whose astral form, as seen floating above his body, was externally little more than a shapeless wreath of mist. It was found that the consciousness of the body on the bed was dull and heavy, both as regarded the grosser and the etheric parts of the frame. The former responded to some extent to external stimuli- for example, the sprinkling of two or three drops of water on the face called up in the brain (though somewhat tardily) a picture of a heavy shower of rain; while the etheric part of the brain was as usual a passive channel for an endless stream of disconnected thoughts, though it rarely responded to any of the vibrations they produced, and even when it did it seemed somewhat sluggish in its action. The ego floating above was an undeveloped and semi-unconscious condition, but the astral envelope, though shapeless and ill-defined, showed considerable activity.

The floating astral can at any time be acted upon, with an ease that can scarcely be imagined, by the conscious thought of another person ; and in this case the experiment was made of withdrawing it to some little distance from the physical body on the bed, with the result, however, that as soon as it was more than a few yards away considerable uneasiness was manifested in both the vehicles, and it became necessary to desist from the attempt, as evidently any further withdrawal would have caused the man to awake, probably in a state of great terror.

A certain scene was chosen- a view of the most magnificent character from the summit of a mountain in the tropics- and a vivid picture of it was projected by the operator into the dreamy consciousness of the ego, which assimilated and examined it, though in a dull, apathetic, and unappreciative kind of way. After this scene had been held before his view for some time the man was awakened, the object being, of course, to see whether he recollected it as a dream. His mind, however, was an absolute blank on the subject, and except for some vague yearnings of the most animal description, he had brought back no memory whatever from the state of sleep. It was suggested that possibly the constant stream of thought-forms from outside, which flowed through his brain, might constitute an obstacle by so distracting it as to make it unreceptive to influences from its higher principles, so after the man had again fallen asleep, a magnetic shell was formed around his body to prevent the entrance of this stream, and the experiment was tried again.

When thus deprived of its ordinary pabulum, his brain began very slowly and dreamily to evolve out of itself scenes of the man's past life; but when he was again aroused, the result was precisely the same- his memory was absolutely blank as to the scene put before him, though he had some vague idea of having dreamed of some event in his past. This subject was then for the time resigned as hopeless, it being fairly evident that his ego was too little developed, and his karmic principle too strong, to give any reasonable probability of success.

Another effort made with the same man at a later period was not quite so utter a failure, the scene put before him in this case being a very exciting incident from the battle-field, which was chosen as being probably more likely to appeal to his type of mind than the landscape. This picture was undoubtedly received by this undeveloped ego with more interest than the other, but still, when the man was awakened the memory was gone, all that remained being an indistinct idea that he had been fighting, but where or why he had quite forgotten. The next subject taken was a person of much higher type- a man of good moral life, educated and intellectual, with broad, philanthropic ideas and exalted ambitions. In his case the denser body responded instantaneously to the water test by a very respectable picture of a tremendous thunderstorm, and that in turn, reacting on the etheric part of the brain, called up by association a whole series of vividly-represented scenes. When this disturbance was over, the usual stream of thoughts began to flow through, but it was observable that a far greater proportion of them awoke a response in this brain- also that the responsive vibrations were much stronger, and that in each case a train of associations was started which sometimes excluded the stream from outside for quite a considerable time.

The astral vehicle in this subject was far more definite in its ovoid outline, and the body of denser astral matter within it was a very fair reproduction of his physical form; and while desire was decidedly less active, the ego itself possessed a much higher grade of consciousness. The astral body in this case could be drawn away to a distance of several miles from the physical without apparently producing the slightest sense of disquiet in either of them. When the tropical landscape was submitted to this ego, he at once seized upon it with the greatest appreciation, admiring and dwelling upon its beauties in the most enthusiastic manner. After letting him admire it for awhile the man was aroused, but the result was somewhat disappointing. He knew that he had had a beautiful dream, but was quite unable to recall any details, the few elusive fragments that were uppermost in his mind being remnants of the ramblings of his own brain.

With him, as with the other man, the experiment was

then repeated with the addition of a magnetic shell thrown round the body, and in this case, as in the other, the brain at once began to evolve pictures of its own. The ego received the landscape with even greater enthusiasm than at first, recognizing it at once as the view he had seen before, and surveying it point by point with quite ecstatic admiration of its many beauties.

But while he was thus engaged in contemplation of it, the etheric brain down below was amusing itself by recalling pictures of his school-life, the most prominent being a scene on a winter day, when the ground was covered with snow, and he and a number of his playmates were snowballing one another in the school playground. When the man was aroused as usual, the effect was exceedingly curious. He had a most vivid remembrance of standing upon the summit of a mountain, admiring a magnificent view, and he even had the main features of the scenery quite clearly in his mind; but instead of the gorgeous tropical verdure which lent such richness to the real prospect, he saw the surrounding country entirely covered with a mantle of snow! And it seemed to him that even while he was drinking in with deep delight the loveliness of the panorama spread out before him, he suddenly found himself, by one of the rapid transitions so frequent in dreams, snowballing with boyhood's long-forgotten companions in the old school-yard, of which he had not thought for years.

CHAPTER VII: CONCLUSION

Surely these experiments show very clearly how the remembrance of our dreams becomes so chaotic and inconsequential as it frequently is. Incidentally they also explain why some people- in whom the ego is undeveloped and earthly desires of various kinds are strong- never dream at all, and why many others are only now and then, under a collocation of favorable circumstances, able to bring back a confused memory of nocturnal adventure; and we see, further, from them that if a man wishes to reap in his waking consciousness the benefit of what his ego may learn during sleep, it is absolutely necessary for him to acquire control over his thoughts, to subdue all lower passions, and to attune his mind to higher things. If he will take the trouble to form during waking life the habit of sustained and concentrated thought, he will soon find that the advantage he gains thereby is not limited to the daytime in its action. Let him learn to hold his mind in check- to show that he is master of that also, as well as of his lower passions; let him patiently labor to acquire absolute control of his thoughts, so that he will always know exactly what he is thinking about, and why, and he will find that his brain, thus trained to listen only to the promptings of the ego, will remain quiescent when not in use, and will decline to receive and respond to casual currents from the surrounding ocean of thought, so that he will no longer be impervious to influences from the less material planes, where insight is keener and judgment truer than they can ever be down here.

The performance of a very elementary act of magic may be of assistance to some people in this training of the etheric part of the brain. The pictures which it evolves for itself (when the thought-stream from outside is shut off) are certainly less likely altogether to prevent the recollection of the ego's experiences, than is the tumultuous rush of that thought-stream itself; so the exclusion of this turbid current, which contains so much more evil than good, is of itself no inconsiderable step towards the desired end. And that much may be accomplished without serious difficulty. Let a man when he lies down to sleep think of the aura which surrounds him; let him will strongly that the outer surface of that aura shall become a shell to protect him from the impingement of influences from without, and the auric matter will obey his thought; a shell will really be formed around him, and the thought-stream will be excluded.

Another point very strongly brought out in our further investigations is the immense importance of the last thought in a man's mind as he sinks to sleep. This is a consideration which never occurs to the vast majority of people at all, yet it affects them physically, mentally, and morally. We have seen how passive and how easily influenced man is during sleep; if he enters that state with his thought fixed upon high and holy things, he thereby draws round him the elementals created by like thought in others; his rest is peaceful, his mind open to impressions from above and closed to those from below, for he has set it working in the right direction. If, on the contrary, he falls asleep with impure and earthly thoughts floating through his brain, he attracts to himself all the gross and evil creatures who come near him, while his sleep is troubled by the wild surgings of passion and desire which render him blind to the sights, deaf to the sounds, that come from higher planes.

All earnest Theosophists should therefore make a special point of raising their thoughts to the loftiest level of which they are capable before allowing themselves to sink into slumber. For remember, through what seem at first but the portals of dream, entrance may perchance presently be gained into those grander realms where alone true vision is possible. If one guides his soul persistently upward, its inner senses will at last begin to unfold; the light within the shrine will burn brighter and brighter, until at last the full continuous consciousness comes, and then he will dream no more. To lie down to sleep will no longer mean for him to sink into oblivion, but simply to step forth radiant, rejoicing, strong, into that fuller, nobler life where fatigue can never come—where the soul is always learning, even though all his time be spent in service; for the service is that of the great Masters of Wisdom, and the glorious task They set before him is to help ever to the fullest limit of his power in Their never-ceasing work for the aiding and the guidance of the evolution of humanity.

DREAMS

THEOSOPHICAL SOCIETY

OBJECTS

To form a nucleus of the universal Brotherhood of Humanity, without distinction of race, creed, sex, caste or color.

To encourage the study of comparative religion, philosophy and science.

To investigate unexplained laws of nature and the powers latent in man.

The Theosophical Society is composed of students, belonging to any religion in the world or to none, who are united by their approval of the above objects, by their wish to remove religious antagonisms and to draw together men of good-will whatsoever their religious opinions, and by their desire to study religious truths and to share the results of their studies with others. Their bond of union is not the profession of a common belief, but a common search and aspiration for Truth. They hold that Truth should be sought by study, by reflection, by purity of life, by devotion to high ideals, and they regard Truth as a prize to be striven for, not as a dogma to be imposed by authority. They consider that belief should be the result of individual study or intuition, and not its antecedent, and should rest on knowledge, not on assertion. They extend tolerance to all, even to the intolerant, not as a privilege they bestow, but as a duty they perform, and they seek to remove ignorance, not to punish it. They see every religion as an expression of the Divine Wisdom, and prefer its study to its condemnation, and its practice to proselytism. Peace is their watch-word, as Truth is their aim.

DREAMS

Theosophy is the body of truths which forms the basis of all religions, and which cannot be claimed as the exclusive possession of any. It offers a philosophy which renders life intelligible, and which demonstrates the justice and the love which guide its evolution.

It puts death in its rightful place, as a recurring incident in an endless life, opening the gateway of a fuller and more radiant existence. It restores to the world the science of the spirit, teaching man to know the spirit as himself, and the mind and body as his servants. It illuminates the scriptures and doctrines of religions by unveiling their hidden meanings, and thus justifying them at the bar of intelligence, as they are ever justified in the eyes of intuition. Members of the Theosophical Society study these truths, and Theosophists endeavor to live them. Every one willing to study, to be tolerant, to aim high, and to work perseveringly, is welcomed as a member, and it rests with the member to become a true Theosophist.

DREAMS

BOOKS RECOMMENDED FOR STUDY

An Outline of Theosophy. C. W. Leadbeater
Ancient Wisdom. Annie Besant
Seven Principles of Man. Annie Besant
Re-incarnation. Annie Besant
Karma. Annie Besant
Death- and After? Annie Besant
The Astral Plane. C. W. Leadbeater
The Devachanic Plane. C. W. Leadbeater
Man and his Bodies. Annie Besant
The Key to Theosophy. H. P. Blavatsky
Esoteric Buddhism. A. P. Sinnett
The Growth of the Soul. A. P. Sinnett
Man's Place in the Universe
Man Visible and Invisible (illustrated). C. W. Leadbeater

A student who has thoroughly mastered these may study
The Secret Doctrine. H. P. Blavatsky. Three volumes and
separate index.

World-Religions

Fragments of a Faith Forgotten. G. R. S. Mead
Esoteric Christianity. Annie Besant
Four Great Religions. Annie Besant
Orpheus. G. R. S. Mead
The Kabalah. A. E. Waite

Ethical

In the Outer Court. Annie Besant
The Path of Discipleship. Annie Besant
The Voice of the Silence. H. P. Blavatsky

DREAMS

Light on the Path. Mabel Collins
Bhagavad-Gita. Trans. Annie Besant
Studies in the Bhagavad-Gita
The Doctrine of the Heart
The Upanishats. Trans; by G. R. S. Mead and J. C. Chattopadyaya.
Three Paths and Dharma. Annie Besant
Theosophy of the Upanishats
The Stanzas of Dzyan. H. P. Blavatsky

Various

Nature's Mysteries. A. P. Sinnett
Clairvoyance. C. W. Leadbeater
Dreams. C. W. Leadbeater
The Building of the Kosmos. Annie Besant
The Evolution of Life and Form. Annie Besant
Some Problems of Life. Annie Besant
Thought-Power, its Control and Culture. Annie Besant
The Science of the Emotions. Bhagavan Das
The Gospel and the Gospels. G. R. S. Mead
Five Years of Theosophy

THE END

Printed in Great Britain
by Amazon